Sharks
Our Ocean Guardians

The Shark Guardian Series Book One

introducing
Jed the Hammerhead

written & illustrated by
Gail Clarke

This book is for shark guardians everywhere and especially for

....(your name)

Dinosaurs lived for millions of years
And left their bones as souvenirs.
Yet in the end there is no doubt
All the dinosaurs died out ...

But in the ocean deep and dark
Lived the prehistoric shark.

Did the sharks die out? No way!
The sharks were really here to stay.
The megalodon, or 'giant tooth',
Survived much longer – that's the truth.

They were creatures of enormous size;
They had giant teeth and watchful eyes.
With their streamlined bodies and powerful tails,
They preyed on squid, large fish and whales!

And even though the megalodon
Is absolutely dead and gone,
He was the same in many ways
As the great white shark we see these days.

In fact it is quite true to say
That all the sharks we see today
Have hardly changed – it now appears –
For a hundred and forty million years.

Shark Features

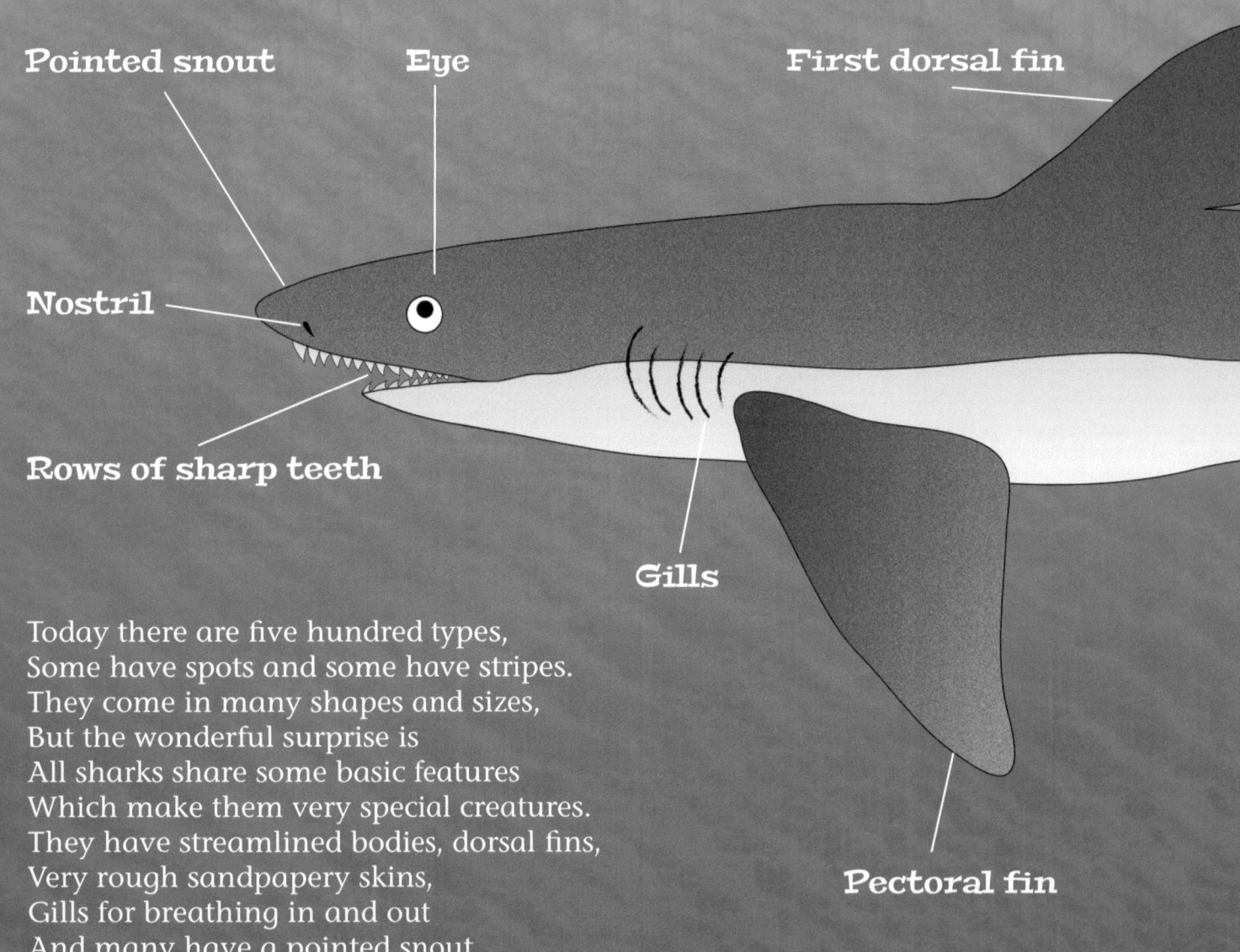

Today there are five hundred types,
Some have spots and some have stripes.
They come in many shapes and sizes,
But the wonderful surprise is
All sharks share some basic features
Which make them very special creatures.
They have streamlined bodies, dorsal fins,
Very rough sandpapery skins,
Gills for breathing in and out
And many have a pointed snout.

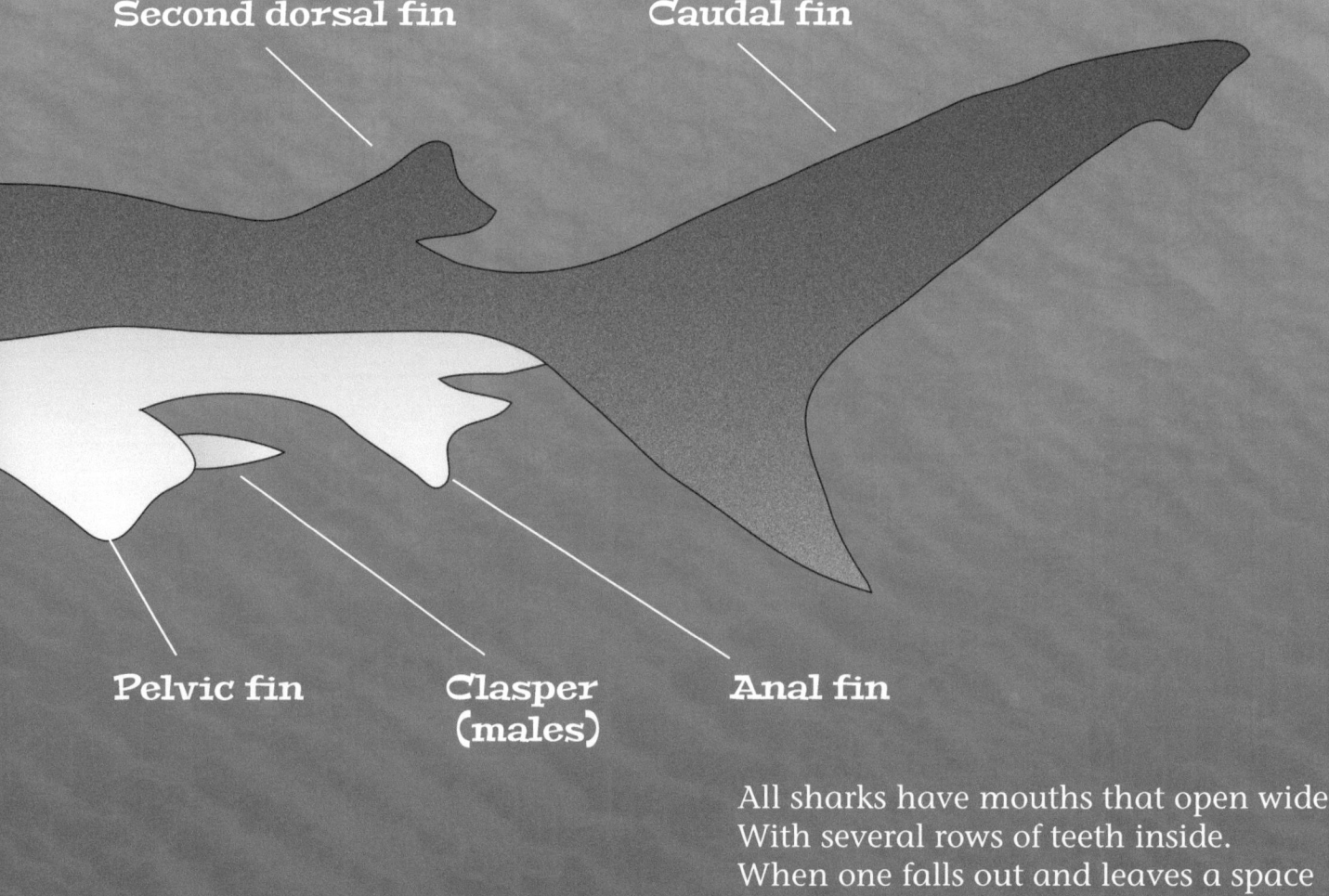

All sharks have mouths that open wide
With several rows of teeth inside.
When one falls out and leaves a space
Another comes to take its place.
And tiny pores help sharks to 'feel'
Where to find a tasty meal.

The Ocean Food Chain

What do sharks eat? Let's explain,
Let's look at the ocean feeding chain.

The sun shines on ocean plants, and so
They very soon begin to grow.

Tiny plankton, shrimps and krill
Eat these plants and have their fill.

Tuna and large fish make a treat
For very hungry sharks to eat.

Not much eats sharks, so they remain
Top of the ocean feeding chain.

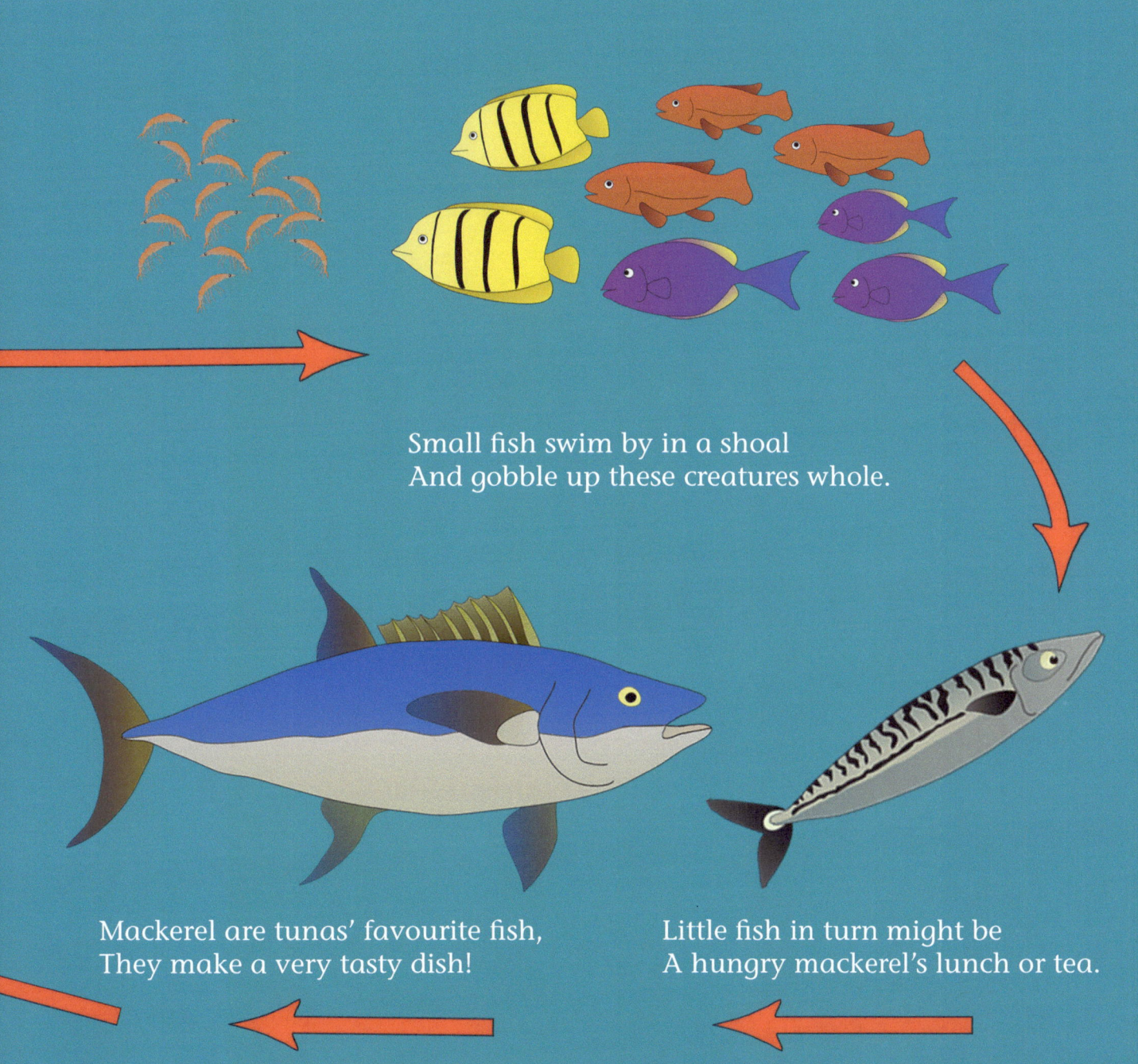

Sharks as Guardians

Since time began sharks have been
Helping to keep our planet clean.
Do you know how much sharks do
To keep our oceans fresh and blue?

Sharks mostly eat the old and slow –
The weakest fish are first to go.
In this way the strong survive –
Only the healthy stay alive.

So it is quite true to say
Sharks are guardians every day.

But who guards the guardians? I'll tell you who:
People like me and people like you,
People like Don and people like Izzy,
Two young Shark Guardians who keep very busy
Touring the planet to show us all how
We can guard the world's sharks
Right here and right now.

We've learned a lot and now it's time
To meet the hero of this rhyme.
He's just been born on the ocean bed;
He's Jed, a scalloped hammerhead.

Mother hammerheads it's true
Don't nurse their young like most mums do.
Each hammerhead is on its own
To hunt and feed and live alone.

Jed's eyes can see both far and wide,
His mouth is on his underside.
He's smart and quick at catching prey
Like squid, small fish and even ray.

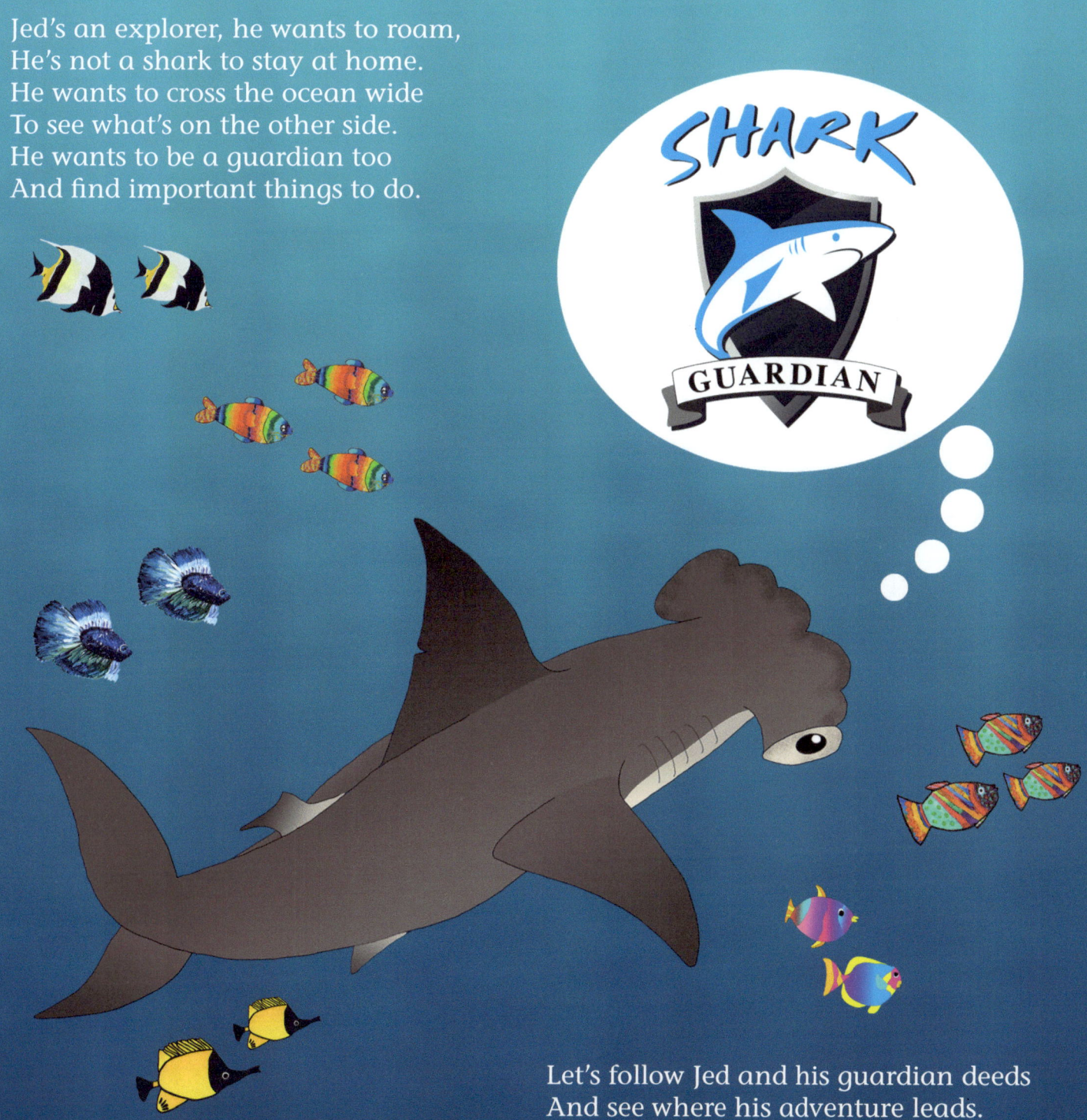

Jed's an explorer, he wants to roam,
He's not a shark to stay at home.
He wants to cross the ocean wide
To see what's on the other side.
He wants to be a guardian too
And find important things to do.

Let's follow Jed and his guardian deeds
And see where his adventure leads.

 # Fascinating Shark Facts

- Megalodon teeth were about 18 cm long.

- The prehistoric helicoprion shark had a spiral of teeth.

- Sharks' eyes are 10 times more sensitive than human eyes.

- Some shark species will drown if they stop moving.

- Some sharks lay eggs. They are called oviparous.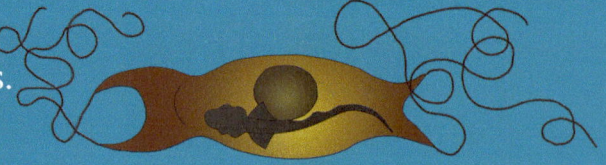

- Some sharks are born looking like their parents. They are called viviparous.

- Most sharks have five gills on each side. Some have six or even more.

- Shark skin is covered with tiny tooth-like scales called dermal denticles that lock together, streamline the shark and help it to swim smoothly.

- The dwarf lantern shark gets its name because it glows in the dark.

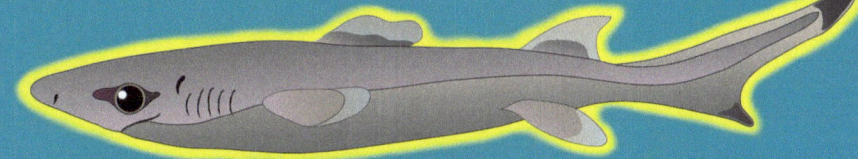

I'm a glow-in-the-dark shark.

- Wobbegongs are strange bearded sharks with incredible camouflaged skin.

Now you see me.

Now you don't.

Jed's Challenge

There are nine different species of hammerhead shark.
Can you find out what their names are?

A Note from Shark Guardian charity directors Brendon Sing & Liz Ward-Sing

Dear Parents and Teachers,

Thank you for supporting Shark Guardian by buying this book.

Shark Guardian is a UK charity which aims to advance the conservation of sharks and many other marine species worldwide for their sustainable management while protecting their natural environment. This is achieved through education, developing skills, conservation activities and promoting research projects.

We are both scuba diving instructors with many years' experience diving with sharks. Since founding the Shark Guardian charity in 2013, our focus has been on educating the next generation of Shark Guardians by inspiring them to help protect shark species worldwide. We hope this book and subsequent books in the series will encourage children to learn more about sharks, to visit oceans in many parts of the world and to discover the extraordinary strength and natural beauty of these amazing creatures.

We are very grateful to children's author and illustrator Gail Clarke for the many hours she has spent putting this book together. It is amazing how she has taken our inspirations and created such a fantastic, factual story with beautiful illustrations.

We are very excited about the next book!

Best wishes,
Liz & Brendon

Find out more about Brendon, Liz, Shark Guardian, sharks and conservation at www.sharkguardian.org

A note from children's author, illustrator and storyteller Gail Clarke

Hi,

I hope you enjoyed this story. I certainly enjoyed writing and illustrating it, and I learned a lot about sharks along the way. Did you learn something too?

This is just the beginning of Jed's ocean adventures. There will be other books in the series in which you can follow Jed's shark guardian deeds as he explores the world's oceans. His mission is to help keep sharks and other marine life safe and healthy.

I have written and illustrated six other books about animals which I have presented to more than thirty-five thousand children around the world. If I haven't already met you, I hope to do so one day!

You can find out more about my books, about writing and illustrating, and about my school visits by looking at my website: www.gailclarkeauthor.com

Copyright © 2019 Gail Clarke
Original text: Gail Clarke, illustrations: Gail Clarke
ISBN 978-1-912406-30-2

All rights reserved
Published by Gupole Publications

Shark Guardian: www.sharkguardian.org
Gail Clarke: www.gailclarkeauthor.com

www.ingramcontent.com/pod-product-compliance
Lightning Source LLC
Chambersburg PA
CBHW042252100526
44587CB00002B/109